Sloths

By Julie Guidone

Reading Consultant: Susan Nations, M.Ed.,
author/literacy coach/consultant in literacy development

WEEKLY READER®
PUBLISHING

Please visit our web site at **www.garethstevens.com**.
For a free catalog describing our list of high-quality books,
call 1-800-542-2595 (USA) or 1-800-387-3178 (Canada).
Our fax: 1-877-542-2596

Library of Congress Cataloging-in-Publication Data

Guidone, Julie.
    Sloths / By Julie Guidone.
        p. cm. — (Animals that live in the rain forest)
    Includes bibliographical references.
    ISBN-10: 1-4339-0026-2   ISBN-13: 978-1-4339-0026-6 (lib. bdg.)
    ISBN-10: 1-4339-0108-0   ISBN-13: 978-1-4339-0108-9 (softcover)
    1. Sloths—Juvenile literature. I. Title.
QL737.E2G85   2009
599.3'13—dc22   2008029037

This edition first published in 2009 by
Weekly Reader® Books
An Imprint of Gareth Stevens Publishing
1 Reader's Digest Road
Pleasantville, NY 10570-7000 USA

Copyright © 2009 by Gareth Stevens, Inc.

Executive Managing Editor: Lisa M. Herrington
Senior Editor: Barbara Bakowski
Creative Director: Lisa Donovan
Designers: Michelle Castro, Alexandria Davis
Photo Researcher: Diane Laska-Swanke
Publisher: Keith Garton

Photo Credits: Cover © Buddy Mays/Corbis; pp. 1, 7, 9, 13, 19 © Michael & Patricia Fogden/Minden
Pictures; p. 5 © Michael & Patricia Fogden/CORBIS; p. 11 © Donald Enright/Alamy; p. 15 © Gerry Ellis/
Minden Pictures; p. 17 © Tui De Roy/Minden Pictures; p. 21 (both) © Ingo Arndt/Foto Natura/
Minden Pictures

Printed in the United States of America

1 2 3 4 5 6 7 8 9 10 09 08

Table of Contents

Boldface words appear in the glossary.

An Upside-Down Life

Sloths are animals that live in the **rain forest**. Rain forests are warm, wet woodlands. Sloths spend most of their lives hanging upside down in trees.

Sloths sleep and eat upside down. They even have their babies in trees. A baby sloth rides along on its mother's stomach.

baby sloth

A sloth is about the size of a large cat. It has long legs and curved **claws**. The claws help the sloth hold on to tree branches.

claws

Leafy Greens

Sloths like to eat leaves. They use their hard lips to bite the leaves. They crush the leaves with teeth in their cheeks.

Leaves do not give a sloth much energy. The sloth moves slowly. It falls asleep upside down with its head tucked close to its body.

Staying Safe

A sloth's long gray-brown hair blends in with the trees. Other animals cannot see the sloth.

hair

Sloths use their sharp claws to fight off **predators**. Large snakes, harpy eagles, and **jaguars** hunt sloths.

harpy eagle

Most predators live on the ground, so sloths stay safe in the trees. On land, they can only crawl slowly. In water, sloths swim very well!

How Many Toes?

All sloths have three toes on their back legs. Two-toed sloths have two toes on their front legs. How many toes do three-toed sloths have on their front legs?

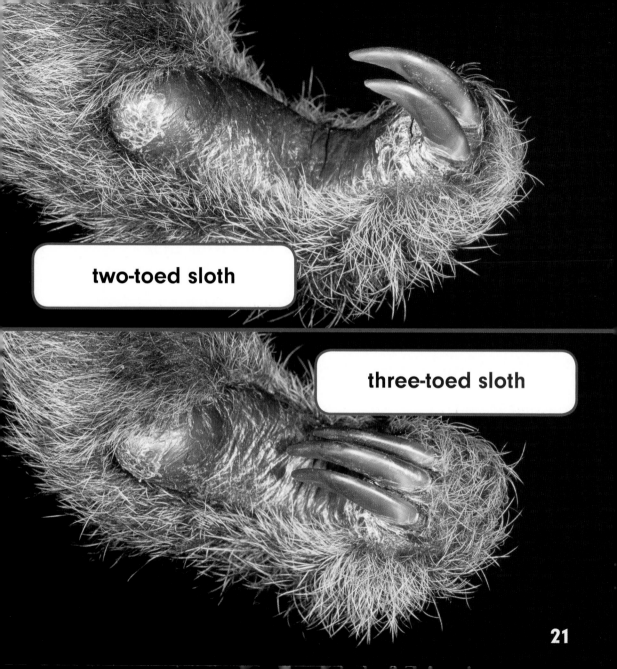

two-toed sloth

three-toed sloth

Glossary

claws: sharp, hooked nails on an animal's foot

jaguars: big cats that live in rain forests

predators: animals that kill and eat other animals

rain forest: a warm, rainy woodland with many types of plants and animals

For More Information

Books

Baby Sloth. Nature Babies (series). Aubrey Lang (Fitzhenry and Whiteside, 2004)

"Slowly, Slowly, Slowly," said the Sloth. Eric Carle (Puffin Books, 2007)

Web Sites

New York Zoos and Aquarium: Sloth Video
nyzoosandaquarium.com/cpz_news/twotoedsloth
Watch Matilda, a two-toed sloth, on the move at the Central Park Zoo.

Sloths at Enchanted Learning
www.enchantedlearning.com/subjects/mammals/sloth
Learn more about sloths, and print a picture to color.

Index

About the Author

Julie Guidone has taught kindergarten and first and second grades in Madison, Connecticut, and Fayetteville, New York. She loves to take her students on field trips to the zoo to learn about all kinds of animals! She lives in Syracuse, New York, with her husband, Chris, and her son, Anthony.